Keto After 50

Lose Up to 7 Pounds in 7 days with The Ketogenic Diet For A Quick Weight Loss With Easy, Tasty and Affordable Recipes.

Ketogenic Lab

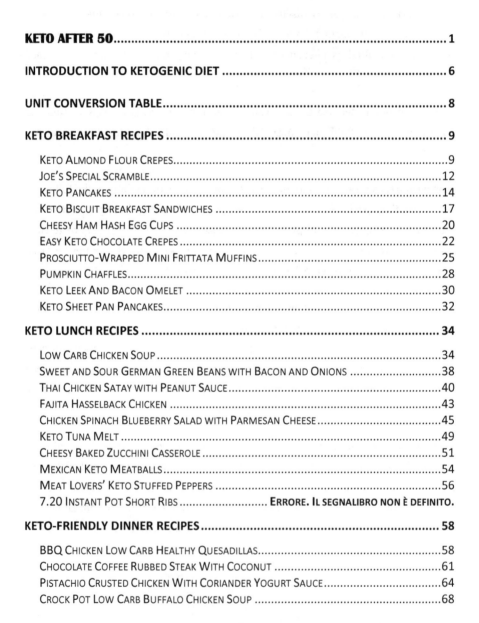

The Keto-OS diet helps to supply the liver with dietary sources of carbohydrates and produces ketones as an energy source for cellular energy. It is known with many names such as Low carb diet, ketogenic diet, low carb high fat (LCHF), etc.

The body produces Insulin and Glucose after the digestion of food with high carb content.

- The easiest molecule to produce in your body is Glucose, and it is used as a source of energy other than any source.
- And to process Glucose all around the body, the main chemical responsible for it is Insulin.

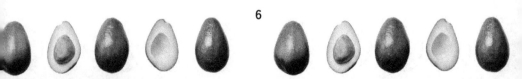

Most importantly, since glucose is the body's primary energy source, the fats are being stored for later use by other functions, such as brain activity and glycogen for exercise. . Glucose usually is the main energy source of the body on a high carb diet. Thus, when you reduce the amount of carbohydrate intake, the body begins a system known as Ketosis.

Ketogenic diet

Carbohydrates	5%
Protein	25%
Fat	70%

Unit Conversion Table

Volume and weight conversions are an important resource to have in the kitchen. When halving or doubling a recipe, making the correct conversions can make or break your final results.

COOKING CONVERSION CHART

Measurement

CUP	ONCES	MILLILITERS	TABLESPOONS
8 cup	64 oz	1895 ml	128
6 cup	48 oz	1420 ml	96
5 cup	40 oz	1180 ml	80
4 cup	32 oz	960 ml	64
2 cup	16 oz	480 ml	32
1 cup	8 oz	240 ml	16
3/4 cup	6 oz	177 ml	12
2/3 cup	5 oz	158 ml	11
1/2 cup	4 oz	118 ml	8
3/8 cup	3 oz	90 ml	6
1/3 cup	2.5 oz	79 ml	5.5
1/4 cup	2 oz	59 ml	4
1/8 cup	1 oz	30 ml	3
1/16 cup	1/2 oz	15 ml	1

Temperature

FAHRENHEIT	CELSIUS
100 °F	37 °C
150 °F	65 °C
200 °F	93 °C
250 °F	121 °C
300 °F	150 °C
325 °F	160 °C
350 °F	180 °C
375 °F	190 °C
400 °F	200 °C
425 °F	220 °C
450 °F	230 °C
500 °F	260 °C
525 °F	274 °C
550 °F	288 °C

Weight

IMPERIAL	METRIC
1/2 oz	15 g
1 oz	29 g
2 oz	57 g
3 oz	85 g
4 oz	113 g
5 oz	141 g
6 oz	170 g
8 oz	227 g
10 oz	283 g
12 oz	340 g
13 oz	369 g
14 oz	397 g
15 oz	425 g
1 lb	453 g

Keto Almond Flour Crepes

Servings: 8 to 10 crepes | Time: 35 mins | Difficulty: Easy

Nutrients per serving: Calories: 158 kcal | Fat: 13g | Carbohydrates: 3.04g | Protein: 6.28g | Fiber: 1.16g

Ingredients

- 4 Eggs

- 1 Tsp. Olive Oil

- 1/2 Cup Cream Cheese, Softened

- 1/4 Cup Almond Milk, Unsweetened

- 2 Tbsps. Swerve Sweetener, Granulated

- 3/4 Cup Almond Flour

- 1/8 Tsp. Salt

Method

1. Combine all the ingredients in a blender, except oil. Blend until a smooth consistency is attained.

2. Heat olive oil in a pan over medium-low flame and put this egg mixture in it. Swirl the pan to spread the batter evenly.

3. Cook both sides to golden brown and dish out.

4. Serve with any low carb spread of your choice.

Joe's Special Scramble

Servings: 4 | Time: 30 mins | Difficulty: Easy

Nutrients per serving: Calories: 403 kcal | Fat: 30g | Carbohydrates: 8g | Protein: 27g | Fiber: 2g

Ingredients

- 2 Tbsps. Avocado Oil

- 3 Garlic Cloves, Minced

- 1 Cup Beef, Ground

- 2/3 Cup Baby Spinach

- 10 Eggs

- 1/2 Cup Onion, Finely Chopped

- 1 Tsp. Red Boat Fish Sauce

- 1 Cup Cremini Mushrooms, Trimmed & Sliced Thinly

- 2 Tbsps. Water

- 2 Tbsps. Chives, Chopped

- Black Pepper, Freshly Ground, To Taste

- Kosher Salt, To Taste

- Cayenne Pepper Sauce (Optional)

Method

1. Combine eggs, fish sauce, salt, and pepper in a bowl and whisk well. Set aside.

2. Heat avocado oil in a skillet over a medium-high flame and sauté onions and mushrooms with a sprinkle of salt. Cook it until the mushrooms become soft and golden brown.

3. Add in the garlic and stir fry it as well until it is fragrant. Then put the ground beef in it and brown it.

4. Add more salt if you want and once the beef is browned, add the spinach, and cook it until it wilts.

5. Pour the egg mixture in it and let it sit for a few minutes and then stir it.

6. Once cooked through, dish it out and serve with hot sauce if you want.

Keto Pancakes

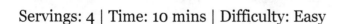

Servings: 4 | Time: 10 mins | Difficulty: Easy

Nutrients per serving: Calories: 395 kcal | Fat: 34g | Carbohydrates: 12g | Protein: 14g | Fiber: 6g

Ingredients

- 1/4 Cup Coconut Flour

- Mixed Berries (Raspberries Strawberries, Blueberries)

- 1/4 Cup Coconut Oil

- 1 Cup Almond Flour

- 1 Tsp. Baking Powder (Gluten-Free)

- 1/3 Cup Almond Milk, Unsweetened

- 5 Eggs

- 1 & 1/2 Tsps. Vanilla Extract

- 2-3 Tbsps. Erythritol

- 1/4 Tsp. Salt

Method

1. Preheat a griddle to 300 degrees.

2. Take a bowl and combine all the ingredients in it. Whisk them well until a smooth mixture is formed.

3. Pour a quarter cup of the batter onto the griddle and cook the pancake from both sides until it becomes golden brown.

4. Repeat the process with the remaining batter.

5. Dish out and serve with a low carb syrup or topping.

Keto Biscuit Breakfast Sandwiches

Servings: 8 | Time: 40 mins | Difficulty: Easy

Nutrients per serving (one biscuit without filling): Calories: 216 kcal | Fat: 6g | Carbohydrates: 6g | Protein: 6g | Fiber: 2g

Ingredients

- 8 Breakfast Sausage Patties, Cooked

- 1 & 1/2 Cups Almond Flour

- 1 Tbsp. Baking Powder (Aluminum Free)

- 4 Tbsps. Butter, Unsalted & Melted

- 8 Slices Cheddar Cheese

- 6 Eggs

- 1/2 Tbsp. Oil

- 3/4 Tsp. Garlic Powder

- 1/2 Cup Sour Cream, Full Fat

- 3/4 Tsp. Onion Powder

- 4 Tbsps. Milk

- Salt, To Taste

- Pepper, To Taste

- Cooking Spray

Method

1. Preheat the oven to 450 degrees F.

2. Combine the almond flour, baking powder, 1/4 tsp salt, onion, and garlic powder in a bowl and whisk well.

3. Combine two eggs, melted butter, and sour cream in another bowl and whisk them together as well.

4. Put the egg mixture in the dry mixture and whisk again until smooth.

5. Take a 12-cup muffin tin and spray it with a cooking spray.

6. Pour 1/4 cup of batter in each cup of the muffin tin and put in the oven.

7. Bake the biscuits until they become golden, for about 10-11 minutes.

8. Take out of the oven once done and allow them to cool down for about 15-20 minutes. Then take them out of the muffin tin and set them aside.

9. Combine four eggs, milk, salt, and butter as per your taste, in a bowl and whisk them well.

10. Heat oil in a pan over medium flame and pour the egg mixture in it. Swirl the pan to evenly spread it.

11. Flip the egg mixture, once cooked from one side, and cook from the other.

12. Once cooked from both sides, remove from the heat ad cut into small squares to fit the biscuits.

13. Cut the biscuits into halves like a sandwich and put the egg squares, cheese sausage patties in between.

Cheesy Ham Hash Egg Cups

Servings: 9 | Time: 35 mins | Difficulty: Easy

Nutrients per serving: Calories: 220 kcal | Fat: 18g | Carbohydrates: 1g | Protein: 15g

Ingredients

- 9 Eggs

- 1/4 Cup Almond Flour

- 2 Cups Ham, Chopped

- 1/3 Cup Mayonnaise, Sugar-Free

- 1/4 Tsp. Garlic Powder

- 1/4 Cup Onion, Chopped

- 1/3 Cup. Parmesan Cheese, Grated

- 1 Tbsp. Parsley, Fresh & Chopped

- 1/4 Tsp. Kosher Salt

- 1/8 Tsp. Black Pepper, Ground

1. Preheat the oven to 375 degrees F.

2. Combine the onion, ham, garlic powder, parsley, salt, and pepper in a food processor and grind them coarsely.

3. Put this mixture in a bowl and add the almond flour, mayonnaise, and parmesan cheese in it. Stir it well to combine.

4. Spray a muffin tray with cooking spray and put the spoonful of this mixture in each muffin cup, leaving a space empty for the egg.

5. Put the tray in the preheated oven and bake for about 5 minutes.

6. Take out of the oven and crack one egg in each cup.

7. Put back in the oven for 15-20 minutes or until the eggs are cooked.

8. Once done, take out and let cool for five minutes, then take out and garnish with parsley before serving.

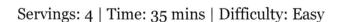

Servings: 4 | Time: 35 mins | Difficulty: Easy

Nutrients per serving: Calories: 186 kcal | Fat: 14.1g | Carbohydrates: 2.2g | Protein: 10.9g

Ingredients

- 4 Eggs

- 3 Tbsps. Coconut Flour

- 2 Tbsps. Cocoa Powder, Dark & Unsweetened

- 1/2 Cup Cream Cheese, Full-Fat

- 1/4 Cup Erythritol, Powdered

- 1 Tsp. Vanilla Extract (Optional)

Method

1. Take a bowl and put all the ingredients in it. Whisk the mixture well until combined.

2. Heat a non-stick pan over medium-low flame and pour a quarter of the mixture in it with a spoon, and spread it evenly with the back of the spoon.

3. Cook on both sides until golden.

4. Repeat the process with the remaining batter.

5. Dish out and serve with whipped cream and berries if you want.

Prosciutto-Wrapped Mini Frittata Muffins

Servings: 12 Muffins | Time: 30 mins | Difficulty: Easy

Nutrients per serving: Calories: 164 kcal | Fat: 14g | Carbohydrates: 4g | Protein: 7g | Fiber: 1g

Ingredients

- 4 Tbsps. Avocado Oil

- 8 Eggs

- 1/4 Cup Coconut Milk, Full-Fat

- 1 Cup Cremini Mushrooms, Sliced Thinly

- 1 Cup Cherry Tomatoes, Halved

- 1 Cup Spinach, Frozen

- 3 Garlic Cloves, Minced

- 2/3 Cup Prosciutto Di Parma

- 1 Cup Onion, Chopped

- Kosher Salt, To Taste

- Black Pepper, Freshly Ground, To Taste

- 2 Tbsps. Coconut Flour

Method

1. Preheat the oven to 375 degrees F.

2. Heat half the avocado oil in a skillet over medium flame and sauté the onions in it until they become translucent. Next, add the garlic and sauté it as well.

3. Add in the mushrooms, spinach, salt, and pepper. Stir fry until the mushroom becomes golden and spinach is wilted.

4. Once done, take out and set aside to let cool.

5. In the meantime, combine the coconut flour, eggs, coconut milk, salt, and pepper in a bowl and whisk them well until the mixture become smooth.

6. Add in the fried veggies mixture and stir well.

7. Take a muffin tin and brush it with the remaining avocado oil. Then line each cup with prosciutto, covering the bottom and sides entirely.

8. Pour a spoonful of frittata batter in each cup and put a tomato half on top.

9. Take out once done and let cool before serving

Pumpkin Chaffles

Servings: 2 Chaffles | Time: 13 mins | Difficulty: Easy

Nutrients per serving: Calories: 116.26 kcal | Fat: 9.54g | Carbohydrates: 2.61g | Protein: 4.52g | Fiber: 0.62g

Ingredients

- 1 Tbsp. Almond Flour

- 1/2 Tsp. Pumpkin Spice

- 1 Large Egg

- 1 Tbsp. Pumpkin Puree

- 2 Tbsps. Cream Cheese, Softened

- 1/4 Tsp. Baking Powder (Optional)

- Cooking Oil Spray

- 1/2 Tsp Erythritol, Granular (Optional)

Method

1. Preheat the waffle iron.

2. Combine all the ingredients in a bowl and whisk well to make a smooth batter.

3. Spray the preheated waffle iron with a cooking oil spray and then pour the batter into it. Close it and let it cook for about 4-5 minutes or until the chaffles are golden brown. Repeat this with the remaining batter and dish out once done.

4. Serve with low carb toppings and enjoy.

Keto Leek And Bacon Omelet

Servings: 4 | Time: 32 mins | Difficulty: Easy

Nutrients per serving: Calories: 124 kcal | Fat: 20g | Carbohydrates: 3g | Protein: 17g

Ingredients

- 2 Tbsps. Avocado Oil

- Sea Salt, To Taste

- 2/3 Cup Bacon, Cooked & Chopped

- Parsley, Fresh and Chopped

- 8 Eggs

- 1 Leek, Sliced

- Black Pepper, Freshly Ground, To Taste

- Chives, Fresh & Minced

<u>Method</u>

1. Combine the eggs with salt and pepper and whisk them.

2. Heat oil in a pan and sauté the leek in it for 5 minutes or until it becomes soft.

3. Add in the beaten egg mixture and chopped bacon.

4. Swirl the pan to evenly spread the eggs. Flip once done from one side and cook both sides for a few minutes.

5. Once cooked, dish out and sprinkle chives and parsley on top.

Keto Sheet Pan Pancakes

Servings: 15 | Time: 30 mins | Difficulty: Easy

Nutrients per serving: Calories: 221 kcal | Fat: 18.7g | Carbohydrates: 7.5g | Protein: 7.5g | Fiber: 4.2g

Ingredients

- 2 Tbsps. Coconut Flour

- 5 Eggs

- 1 Tbsp. Baking Powder

- 1 Cup Coconut Or Almond Milk

- 2 Tsps. Vanilla Extract

- 6 Tbsps. Butter, Melted

- 3 Cups Almond Flour

- 1/2 Tsp. Salt

- 6 Tbsps. Swerve Sweetener

- Cooking Spray

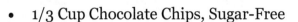

- 1/3 Cup Chocolate Chips, Sugar-Free

Method

1. Preheat the oven to 400 degrees F.

2. Combine all the ingredients in a large bowl except the chocolate chips. Whisk or beat it well until a smooth batter is formed.

3. Line a baking pan (11x17 inches) with parchment paper and spray it with cooking spray. Pour the batter in it and sprinkle the chocolate chips on top.

4. Put the pan in the preheated oven and bake for about 12 to 15 minutes or until the edges become golden and the center firm.

5. Take out of the oven once done and let cool for a few minutes.

6. Cut into 15 large squares and serve.

Low Carb Chicken Soup

Servings: 6 | Time: 30 mins | Difficulty: Easy

Nutrients per serving: Calories: 274 kcal | Fat: 15g | Carbohydrates: 8g | Protein: 26g | Fiber: 2g

Ingredients

- 6 cups bone broth

- 2 cups cooked chicken, diced

Vegetable Base

- 1 cup celery, sliced

- 4 tbsp butter, avocado oil, or olive oil

- 1/2 cup onion, diced

- 1 large garlic clove, sliced

- 8 ounces celery root, cubed

- 1 whole bay leaf

- 1/3 cup carrot

- 2 tsp chicken base

- 1 tsp lemon zest

- 2 tsp lemon juice mixed with water

- salt and pepper to taste

- 1 tbsp garlic herb seasoning blend

- 1/4 cup dry white wine

Method

1. Take diced chicken.

2. Take vegetables. Peel and cut them.

3. Add butter, lemon zest, bay leaf, and vegetables in a quart pot on medium heat.

4. Stir continuously to coat everything.

5. Add chicken base, wine, and garlic herb blend after reducing the heat to medium.

6. Cook vegetables for about 3-4 minutes until they turn brown.

7. Boil the chicken broth, then simmer the vegetables over reduced heat until they become tender. Add the chicken broth and bring it to just under a boil.

8. Add pepper and salt to taste.

Sweet and Sour German Green Beans with Bacon and Onions

Servings: 4 | Time: 18 mins | Difficulty: Easy

Nutrients per serving: Calories: 166 kcal | Fat: 11g | Carbohydrates: 8g | Protein: 9g | Fiber: 4g

Ingredients

- 4 slices bacon, diced

- 2 cups green beans

- 2 tbsp apple cider vinegar

- 1/4 cup onion, finely chopped

- 1 tbsp Low carb brown sugar

- 2 tbsp water

- 1 tsp wholegrain mustard

- 1/4 tsp salt

Method

1. Take trimmed beans, chopped onions, and diced bacon.

2. Turn beans tender by cooking.

3. Cook bacon in a pan over medium heat for 4 minutes.

4. Sauté the onions.

5. Add the Sukrin Gold, water, onions, and cider vinegar to the bacon.

6. Take a pan and put grain mustard in it.

7. At last, take green beans and coat by stirring at heat thoroughly.

8. Use pepper and salt to taste.

Thai Chicken Satay with Peanut Sauce

Servings: 4 | Time: 35 mins | Difficulty: Easy

Nutrients per serving: Calories: 279 kcal | Fat: 15g | Carbohydrates: 4g | Protein: 30g | Fiber: 1g

Ingredients

- 2 cups chicken tenders

Chicken Satay Marinade

- 1 tbsp Hot Madras Curry Powder

- 1/3 cup full fat coconut milk from a can

- 1/4 cup chopped fresh cilantro (optional)

- 1/2 tsp ground coriander

- 2 tbsp Red Boat Fish Sauce (optional)

- 2 tbsp Low carb brown sugar

Peanut Sauce

- 1/3 cup full fat coconut milk from a can

- 1 tsp soy sauce

- 1/4 cup smooth peanut/almond butter

- 1-2 tsp chile-garlic sauce

- 1 tbsp Low carb brown sugar

- 1/2 tsp Thai Red Curry Paste

Extras

- soaked bamboo skewers

- lime wedges

- chopped fresh cilantro

Method

1. take warm water and soak the skewers in it.

2. Cut the chicken in half and place it in zip-lock bags.

3. Take the satay marinade in a bowl and put a chicken in it to coat all sides of the chicken.

4. Marinate overnight or for 30 minutes.

5. Warm peanut butter in a small bowl.

6. Whisk in the chile-garlic sauce, Sukrin Gold, Thai curry paste, and soy sauce.

7. Then, add coconut milk slowly.

8. Season it to taste.

9. Refrigerate it.

10. Thread the chicken tenders onto the bamboo skewers.

11. Cook the chicken on the grill, either indoor or outdoor.

12. Garnish it with fresh cilantro (chopped).

13. Serve with the peanut sauce and a lime wedge.

Fajita Hasselback Chicken

Servings: 4 | Time: 5 mins | Difficulty: Easy

Nutrients per serving: Calories: 368 kcal | Fat: 11g | Carbohydrates: 9g | Protein: 53g | Fiber: 1g

Ingredients

- ½ red bell pepper, diced

- 4 chicken breasts

- ½ yellow bell pepper, diced

- ½ onion, diced

- 2 Tbsps. fajita spice mix

- ½ cup cheddar cheese (50 g), grated

- 3 Tbsps. salsa

- ½ green pepper, diced

Method

1. Take the oven to 350°F.

2. Cut and slice the chicken but not deep enough to keep the bottom intact.

3. Take fajita mix, and mix the cooked onions and pepper on medium heat.

4. Take salsa and stir in the mixture. Use cheese to sprinkle over it.

5. Melt the cheese and mix all ingredients.

6. Fill chicken slices with 1 tbsp of mixture.

7. Bake the chicken in the oven for 20 minutes, and juice run through it.

Chicken Spinach Blueberry Salad with Parmesan Cheese

Servings: 2 | Time: 20 mins | Difficulty: Easy

Nutrients per serving: Calories: 519 kcal | Fat: 38g | Carbohydrates: 10g | Protein: 35g | Fiber: 4g

Ingredients

Chicken Spinach Blueberry Salad

- 6 cups baby spinach (170 g)

- 8 ounces chicken tenders or chicken breast

- 4 cups fresh blueberries

- Two slices of red onion (paper-thin)

- 2 cups shaved Parmesan cheese

- 1 cup sliced almonds (toasted or raw)

Balsamic Dressing

- 1 tbsp red wine vinegar

- 1/4 cup extra light olive oil

- 1 tbsp balsamic vinegar

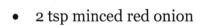

- 2 tsp minced red onion

- 1/2 tsp dijon mustard

- 1 tbsp water

- 1 pinch each salt and pepper

- 1/8 tsp dried thyme

- 1/2 tsp low carb sugar

Method

1. Grill the chicken thoroughly. And cut it into small pieces.

2. Take almonds, and minced the onions, and make the dressing (balsamic).

3. Brown the almonds slightly in a frying pan. Cool it after removing it from the pan.

4. Add all ingredients of the dressing and blend them well with a stick blender.

5. Take spinach and arrange it evenly on two plates.

Keto Tuna Melt

Servings: 4 | Time: 15 mins | Difficulty: Easy

Nutrients per serving: Calories: 227 kcal | Fat: 14g | Carbohydrates: 3g | Protein: 21g | Fiber: 1g

Ingredients

- 3 Tbsps. Mayonnaise

- 1.5 cups Canned Tuna

- ¼ cup Sliced celery

- 1 Tbsp. Finely diced red onion

- 4 slices Cheddar Cheese

- 2 Tbsps. Dill pickle relish

- ¼ Tsp. Salt

- 4 Tomato slices from a large tomato

1. Take a bowl. Add and stir mayonnaise, tuna, celery, red onion, and dill relish.

2. Sprinkle some salt on the tomato slices placed on a baking sheet.

3. Then, on each slice, add 1/4 of the tuna mixture.

4. Take slices of cheese to top each tomato slice.

5. Cook until cheese melts. It should take about 3-5 minutes.

6. Serve

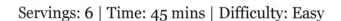

Servings: 6 | Time: 45 mins | Difficulty: Easy

Nutrients per serving: Calories: 275 kcal | Fat: 21g | Carbohydrates: 7g | Protein: 13g | Fiber: 1g

Ingredients

- 2 Tbsps. Butter

- 4.5 cups (approximately) zucchini, large, sliced 1/4 inch thick

- 1/2 cups Onion, diced

- 1 Tsp. Salt

- 1/2 cups Parmesan Cheese, grated and divided

- ½ cup Heavy Cream

- 2 cloves garlic, minced

- 1/2 cups Gruyere Cheese, grated and divided

Method

1. Heat the oven to 450°F.

2. Prepare and pace the salted zucchini slices on a paper towel.

3. Let sit each side for 15 minutes each.

4. Put zucchini slices on a dish.

5. Take a skillet and heat the butter to melt it.

6. Then add onion and garlic to cook them for 3 minutes and 2 minutes, respectively.

7. Add the heavy cream while stirring in a pan.

8. Add Gruyere cheese and Parmesan cheese and melt the cheese while stirring.

9. Add the sauce (cheese) to the zucchini.

10. Bake zucchini with parmesan and Gruyere for 5 minutes by covering the casserole dish with a foil. Remove it when tender.

11. Serve.

Mexican Keto Meatballs

Servings: 15 meatballs| Time: 50 mins | Difficulty: Easy

Nutrients per serving (2 meatballs): Calories: 220 kcal | Fat: 18g | Carbohydrates: 2g | Protein: 14g | Fiber: 2g

Ingredients

- 2 Tbsps. Chili Powder

- 2 Tsps. Salt

- 2 Tbsps. Cumin

- 2 cups Ground Beef

- 1/4 cup Jalapenos, finely diced

- 1 Egg

- 85 g Cheddar Cheese, shredded

1. Take oven to 400°F.

2. Take a large bowl and mix every ingredient in it.

3. Bake balls of 2-inch size after rolling meat in balls like shape.

4. For 25-30 minutes, bake them on a sheet (baking).

Meat Lovers' Keto Stuffed Peppers

Servings: 6 | Time: 1 hr 10 mins | Difficulty: Easy

Nutrients per serving: Calories: 284 kcal | Fat: 22g | Carbohydrates: 6g | Protein: 16g | Fiber: 2g

Ingredients

- 225 g Mozzarella cheese

- 50 g Pepperoni small pieces

- 3 Bell peppers, any color

- ¾ cup Pasta sauce

- Cooked 175 g Italian sausage

Method

1. Heat oven to 400°F.

2. Cut pepper and place them on the dish after removing seeds in them.

3. On the bottom side of each pepper, put 1 tbsp. Sauce.

4. Use pepperoni pieces and 30 g of Italian sausage as a topping.

5. Put some mozzarella.

6. Put sauce, pepperoni, and mozzarella again as the topping. Make sure to fill pepper with enough mozzarella.

7. Bake peppers in the oven for 40 minutes until cheese is melted.

BBQ Chicken Low Carb Healthy Quesadillas

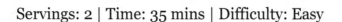

Servings: 2 | Time: 35 mins | Difficulty: Easy

Nutrients per serving: Calories: 459 kcal | Fat: 14.4g | Carbohydrates: 19.5g | Protein: 59.2g | Fiber: 7g

Ingredients

- 1 Cup shredded Chicken breast

- 2 Cups Liquid Egg whites

- Avocado Oil Spray

- 1/4 cup BBQ sauce of choice + extra for drizzling

- 2-4 Tbsp Coriander chopped

- 2/3 cup grated Cheddar cheese

Method

1. Carry a tiny pot of salted water to a simmer, & cook the chicken breast for around 10-15 mins till it is no longer pink inside.

2. Preheat the broiler & adjust the oven rack from the top position to the 2nd position. Use Avocado Oil to spray a cookie sheet.

3. Spray a tiny skillet with Avocado Oil & heat over high heat. Lower the heat when hot, & slowly place a half cup of the white egg in. Cover & cook till just set, around five min, on top of the white egg. Slide the "tortilla" egg on the prepared cookie sheet, & repeat till you have four "tortillas" with the leftover egg whites. Put all the tortillas on the cookie sheet & spray with Avocado Oil on top of them.

4. Cut the chicken using two forks, then put it in a bowl. Please put it in the BBQ sauce till the chicken is very well covered.

5. Split the shredded chicken into two of the "tortillas" then stretch out to surround the "tortilla." Split on top of the chicken, the cheese & Coriander, & spray with avocado oil. Cover with the extra tortillas, the un-cooked egg white side down. With Avocado Oil, brush the tops of the quesadillas.

6. Put the quesadillas underneath the broiler & broil for around fifteen min, till slightly crisp as well as the egg whites start to bubble.

Chocolate Coffee Rubbed Steak With

Coconut

Servings: 2 | Time: 20 mins | Difficulty: Easy

Nutrients per serving: Calories: 286 kcal | Fat: 19g | Carbohydrates: 5g | Protein: 24g | Fiber: 1g

Ingredients

- 1/4 tsp Salt

- 1 tsp ground coffee

- 1/4 tsp Garlic powder

- 1/2 tsp Chili powder

- 1/4 tsp Onion powder

- 1/2 tsp smoked paprika

- 1 tsp cocoa powder, Unsweetened

- 1/8 tsp Cinnamon

- 1 tsp sugar of coconut

- Pepper Pinch

- 2 Tbsp coconut flakes, Unsweetened

- 1/2 Lb Strip steak, New York

Method

1. Combine the ingredients of the rub in a med bowl & set aside.

2. Cut the steak off some big, noticeable chunks of fat & cover it with the rub. Get in there for good to ensure that the steak is properly covered.

3. Cover your steak & let it stay in the fridge for at least one hour, ideally longer to incorporate the flavor.

4. Spray with cooking spray on a grill skillet (or normal pan) & preheat over high heat. Oven preheated to 400 degrees as well.

5. Cook the steak, around 1-2 mins per side, till pleasant & seared on either side.

6. Switch the heat down to med and continue cooking till the appropriate amount of done-ness is met

7. Move to a plate after the steak is cooked & cover this with tinfoil to sit for 5-7 mins.

8. Toast the coconut flakes on a tiny, bakery release paper lined cookie tray whereas the steak is resting. See carefully as it requires just 2 min for them to get soft & golden.

9. Enjoy your steak garnished with a flake of coconut.

Pistachio Crusted Chicken With Coriander

Yogurt Sauce

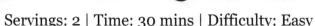

Servings: 2 | Time: 30 mins | Difficulty: Easy

Nutrients per serving: Calories: 409 kcal | Fat: 11g | Carbohydrates: 21g | Protein: 51g | Fiber: 7g

Ingredients

For The Chicken

- Salt

- 1/2 Cup Roasted Pistachios

- 8 Oz Chicken

- One big egg white

    For The Cauliflower Rice

- 4 Cups Cauliflower (cut into bite-sized slices)

- 1/2 cup Coriander, roughly minced

- Salt & pepper

- Fresh juice of a lime, to taste

    For The Sauce

- 1/2 tsp Ground cilantro

- 1/2 cup non-fat Greek yogurt

- 1/8 tsp Cayenne pepper

- Juice of half a lime

- Salt Pinch

Method

1. Oven preheated to 425 degrees & put it on top of a wide cookie sheet with a little cooling rack.

2. Grind your pistachios & a salt pinch in a tiny food processor till the pistachios are processed but still a little bit chunky. This preserves the crunchy chicken. Place the pistachios into a dish with shallow sides. Put the white egg in a med dish.

3. Pat your chicken to dry & put in the white egg, shaking off all the surplus. After this, roll about softly, put in the pistachios, so the full chicken is coated, pressing firmly to stick the nuts to a chicken. Put it on the rack & bake for around 12-15 mins till the chicken is no further pink from the inside, & the outside becomes golden brown & crunchy.

4. Put the cauliflower in a big food processor, whereas the chicken cooks & processes till it appears like rice.

5. Put in a big bowl & microwave the cauliflower rice till tender, around 3-4 mins. Combine with the Coriander & sprinkle to taste with the salt & new lime juice. Place aside

6. In a tiny bowl, mix all the sauce ingredients & serve on top of the chicken & rice of cauliflower.

7. Decorate with it, Coriander.

Crock Pot Low Carb Buffalo Chicken Soup

Servings: 4 | Time: 4 hrs 10 mins | Difficulty: Easy

Nutrients per serving: Calories: 305 kcal | Fat: 26.2g | Carbohydrates: 6.9g | Protein: 11.9g | Fiber: 0.6g

Ingredients

- 3/4 cup thinly sliced Celery

- 1/2 Tbsp Ghee

- 1/4 cup diced Onion

- 2 cups chicken broth (Low-sodium)

- 1/2 cup coconut milk (Full fat)

- 1/4 Cup Hot sauce

- 1/2 Cup full 30 Ranch dressing

- 1/2 tsp Sea salt

- 1/2 Lb Chicken thighs

- 1/4 tsp Paprika

- sliced Green Onion for garnish

- 1 Tbsp Tapioca starch

Method

1. Warm the ghee on med-high heat in a wide bowl. Put in the celery & onion, then cook for around 3-4 mins before they start to soften & brown. Put into the 7-quart crockpot.

2. Cover the chicken with all the leftover ingredients & stir till mixed—Nestle your chicken into a liquid, on HIGH, cover & cook for three hrs.

3. Stir together the tapioca starch & 2 teaspoons of the liquid of cooking in a med bowl till smooth. Mix it back into the crockpot to ensure that it's smooth & blended—Cook for 1 to 2 more hours, or till the soup hardens a bit.

4. Remove & chop the chicken from your crockpot. Through the crockpot, mix it back.

5. Serve it with onion

Cauliflower Fried Rice

Servings: 2 | Time: 20 mins | Difficulty: Easy

Nutrients per serving: Calories: 236 kcal | Fat: 11.4g | Carbohydrates: 24.5g | Protein: 11.8g | Fiber: 6.1g

Ingredients

- 2 Slices smoked bacon (Thick-cut)

- 3/4 cup diced Onion

- 4 Cups Cauliflower florets

- 1 Tbsp minced Garlic

- 1/2 cup sliced Green Onion plus extra for garnish

- 2 Tbsp Water

- 1 Egg

- 2 1/2 Tbsp Coconut aminos

- Salt and pepper to taste

- 1/2 Tbsp sesame oil (Cold-pressed)

- Sesame seeds for garnish

Method

1. On med heat, heat a broad wok & cook the bacon till brown & crispy golden, turning once. Remove to a lined paper-towel plate & pat the extra fat off. Set that bacon fat in the skillet aside.

2. Put the cauliflower florets in a broad food processor as the bacon cooks, and pulsate till rice-like. Place aside

3. 3. Lower the heat to med/high when the bacon is cooked & removed from the grill, & put the onions & garlic. Cook till slightly becomes golden brown, for 1 min.

4. Put the riced cauliflower along with the green onions sliced & cook for around 5 mins, stirring regularly, till the cauliflower becomes golden brown & soft.

5. Heat a tiny non-stick skillet on med heat as the cauliflower cooks. Mix the water with the egg & put it in the skillet. Use a cap to protect & cook till the egg is ready. Don't scramble around it. Cut it onto a chopping board till cooked & break it into small slices.

6. Take it from the heat & stir in the cut egg, coconut amino & sesame oil till the cauliflower is fried. Season with salt & pepper. After this, crumble & whisk in the fried bacon till fairly combined.

7. Decorate with additional sesame & onion seeds.

Coconut Chicken Curry

Servings: 6 | Time: 40 mins | Difficulty: Easy

Nutrients per serving: Calories: 660 kcal | Fat: 60g | Carbohydrates: 7g | Protein: 13g | Fiber: 7g

Ingredients

- 2 Tbsp divided Coconut oil

- 1 1/2 lbs chicken thighs (boneless skinless)

- One thinly sliced Red pepper

- 1/2 cup diced Onion

- 1/2 Tbsp minced fresh garlic

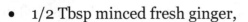

- 1/2 Tbsp minced fresh ginger,

- 2 tsp Turmeric

- 4 tsp yellow curry powder

- 1 tsp ground cumin

- 1 tsp Salt

- 1 tsp Garam masala

- 1 1/2 Cups Chopped tomatoes

- 1 Can coconut milk Full fat (14 oz)

- 1/2 cup minced Coriander

- Rice/cauliflower rice for serving

Method

1. Heat 1 tablespoon of coconut oil on med/high heat in a big, high-sided frying skillet. Include the chicken thighs & cook till seared & golden brown for 1-two min on each side, then move to a tray.

2. The residual oil is applied as well as the heat is switched to med. Put the onion, red pepper, garlic, curry powder, ginger, garam masala & turmeric, then simmer for around five min, till the vegetables start to soften.

3. Put the Coriander to the remaining ingredients, & bring to a simmer. After this cover, boil for 3 mins, lower the heat & boil for ten min. Uncover & cook for another 5-ten min till the sauce has thickened significantly.

4. Take the chicken to a chopping board & chop2 it with two forks, then, together with the Coriander, mix it back into the curry.

5. Serve with the preferred rice.

Low Carb Keto Chicken Stir Fry

Servings: 2 | Time: 25 mins | Difficulty: Easy

Nutrients per serving: Calories: 238 kcal | Fat: 9.6g | Carbohydrates: 15g | Protein: 27g | Fiber: 4.3g

Ingredients

- 1 1/2 Tbsp divided Olive oil

- 1/2 Lb thinly sliced chicken breast (boneless skinless)

- 1/2 courgette Sliced

- One thinly sliced Red pepper

- 1/4 sliced Onion

- 1/2 tsp minced fresh ginger

- 1/2 tsp minced fresh garlic

- 2 Tbsp soy sauce (reduced sodium)

- 1/2 Tbsp Rice vinegar

- Salt

- 1/2 tsp Sesame oil

- Cauliflower rice for serving

- Green onion for garnish

Method

1. In a wide, elevated side skillet or wok, heat one tablespoon of oil over med/high heat. Cook the chicken for around 5-6 mins, till the center is golden brown & no further pink. Move to the skillet.

2. In the skillet, Put the leftover oil & switch the heat to a med amount. Put all the vegetables into the soy sauce & cook for around 5-8 mins, till the vegetables are brown & soft.

3. Return to the chicken & the sesame oil, rice vinegar & soy sauce to the skillet & cook for around 30 sec.

4. Garnish it with green onion & Serve with rice or cauliflower.

Cilantro Lime Cauliflower Rice

Servings: 4 | Time: 20 mins | Difficulty: Easy

Nutrients per serving: Calories: 113.2 kcal | Fat: 7.1g | Carbohydrates: 11.7g | Protein: 3.4g | Fiber: 4.4g

Ingredients

- 2/3 cup diced Onion

- 2 Tbsp Olive oil

- One big head of cauliflower, riced

- 1 Lime juice

- 1/2 tsp Sea salt

- 1/2 cup roughly chopped Coriander

Method

1. In a wide saucepan, heat olive oil to med-high, add onion & cook till soft & slightly browned, around 2-3 mins.

2. Put the cauliflower rice & cook for around 5-6 mins, constantly stirring, till tender & brown.

3. Remove & mix in the salt & juice of lime from the heat. Put it all back on the heat & simmer for another 1-2 mins till a little bit of rice dries out.

4. Change the salt & lime to taste.

Dairy-Free Paleo Casserole With Chicken

Servings: 4 | Time: 1 hr 15 mins | Difficulty: Easy

Nutrients per serving: Calories: 321 kcal | Fat: 19.8g | Carbohydrates: 13.9g | Protein: 25.2g | Fiber: 4g

Ingredients

The Casserole:

- 1 Tbsp plus 1 tsp divided Olive oil

- 1 Lb Lean Ground turkey

- 1/2 cup diced onion

- Pepper

- 1/4 cup plus 2 Tbsp Tomato paste

- One big sliced courgette 1/4 thick

- 1 tsp minced Garlic

- 1/2 tsp Salt

- 1/8 tsp Cardamom powder

- 1/8 tsp Oregano flakes

- 1/4 tsp Cumin powder

- 1/4 tsp Chili powder

- 1/2 tsp minced Fresh Tarragon plus extra for garnish

- 1 big thinly sliced tomato

- 1 cup diced orange bell pepper

   For The Sauce:

- 1 1/2 Tbsp Olive oil

- 1 Tbsp plus 1 tsp Coconut flour

- 1 Tbsp plus 1 tsp Almond meal

- 1 cup Almond milk Unsweetened

- Salt & pepper

Method

1. oven preheated to 350 degrees & spray the olive oil with an 8x8 inch skillet. Place aside

2. Heat 1 Tablespoon of olive oil on med heat in a big saucepan.

3. 3. Put the turkey & roast till it's no further pink, & the outside is soft & brown. Put the minced tomato paste & onion, then sprinkle with salt.

4. Put the sliced courgette and toss with the leftover tsp of olive oil & garlic in a wide bowl. Stir together the cumin, salt, cardamom, chili powder & oregano in a different, shallow bowl. Put & throw in the courgette, ensuring that the spices are uniformly covered.

5. Scatter the courgette on the bottom of the prepared skillet and scatter the fresh tarragon on the rest of the skillet.

6. On top of the courgette, scoop the turkey combination & push back so the turkey is soft & wrapped. Place the sliced tomato with an even layer on the turkey top. Finish by splashing the sliced bell pepper uniformly over the surface of the tomato.

7. Cover and bake the casserole for 15 minutes.

8. Create the sauce as the casserole bakes by boiling the olive oil over medium/high heat in a wide skillet.

9. Put flour of coconut & almond meal, then simmer till the flour begins to soak into the oil & give a dark brown color for around 1 min. Think of black peanut butter.

10. Put in the milk of almond, put it to a boil & whisk continuously. Decrease the heat to mild until boiling so that the sauce remains at a steady low simmer. To make sure it does not smoke, stir regularly.

11. Cook for around 10-11 mins, till the sauce starts to thicken. With salt & pepper, season.

12. Place the sauce uniformly till the casserole is cooked & roast, exposed, for another 45 mins.

13. Let sit for 10 mins; after this slice, Put extra tarragon & enjoy it.

Chicken Pesto Spaghetti Squash

Servings: 2 | Time: 1 hr 15 mins | Difficulty: Easy

Nutrients per serving: Calories: 515 kcal | Fat: 37g |
Carbohydrates: 19g | Protein: 31g | Fiber: 4.6g

Ingredients

- 1 Med spaghetti squash

- 1 Tbsp divided Oil

- 8 Oz cubed chicken breast, Boneless & skinless

- Salt

- Onion powder

- Garlic powder

  The Pesto:

- 2 cups lightly packed Basil (32g)

- 6 Tbsp Pine nuts

- 1 tsp minced fresh garlic

- 1 Tbsp fresh lemon juice

- 2 Tbsp Olive oil

- 1/2 tsp Salt

Method

1. Heat the oven to 400 degrees & use aluminum foil to cover a rimmed cookie sheet.

2. Break the half-length spaghetti squash carefully & scoop out all the seeds. With 1/2 Tablespoon of oil, massage the inside & season with salt. Put on the cookie sheet, cut-side-down, & bake till the fork is soft, approximately 45 minutes to 1 hour. Additionally, on a small cookie sheet, scatter the pine nuts & bake till about golden brown, around 5-10 mins.

3. Heat another 1/2 Tablespoon of oil in a wide pan over low heat until the squash is finished. Sprinkle garlic powder, onion powder & salt on the chicken cubes & simmer for around five min, till golden brown.

Make the Pesto

1. In a Tiny food processor, place the pine nuts & pulse till broken. Put in all the leftover ingredients, excluding the oil, then scrape the sides if required when mixed.

2. With the food processor going, once well mixed, stream in the liquid.

3. Split the squash into Two bowls & combine each squash with 1/2 of the pesto. If needed, finish with chicken & extra sliced Basil. Sprinkle with salt to taste.

Blueberry Banana Bread Smoothie

Servings: 2 | Time: 10 mins | Difficulty: Easy

Nutrients per serving: Calories: 270 kcal | Fat: 23.31g | Carbohydrates: 4.66g | Protein: 3.13g | Fiber: 5.65g

Ingredients

- 1/4 Cup Blueberries

- 2 Tbsps. MCT Oil

- 2 1 & 1/2 Tsps. Banana Extract

- Cups Vanilla Coconut Milk, Unsweetened

- 1 Tbsp. Chia Seeds

- 3 Tbsps. Golden Flaxseed Meal

- 10 Drop Liquid Stevia

- 1/4 Tsp. Xanthan Gum

Method

1. Combine all the ingredients in a blender and let it sit for a few minutes to allow the chia and flax seeds to soak some moisture.

2. Then blend for a minute or two until a smooth consistency is attained.

3. Serve in the glasses and enjoy.

Blackberry Chocolate Shake

Servings: 2 | Time: 5 mins | Difficulty: Easy

Nutrients per serving: Calories: 346 kcal | Fat: 34.17g | Carbohydrates: 4.8g | Protein: 2.62g | Fiber: 7.4g

Ingredients

- 1/4 Cup Blackberries

- 2 Tbsps. MCT Oil

- 1 Cup Coconut Milk, Unsweetened

- 1/4 Tsp. Xanthan Gum

- 2 Tbsps. Cocoa Powder

- 12 Drops Liquid Stevia

- 7 Ice Cubes

Method

1. Combine all the ingredients in a blender and blend for a minute or two until a smooth consistency is attained.

2. Serve in the glasses and enjoy.

Dairy-Free Dark Chocolate Shake

Servings: 2 | Time: 5 mins | Difficulty: Easy

Nutrients per serving: Calories: 349.35 kcal | Fat: 33.15g | Carbohydrates: 5.73g | Protein: 7.2g | Fiber: 6.1g

Ingredients

- 1/2 Avocado

- 1/2 Cup Coconut Cream, Chilled

- 2 Tbsps. Hulled Hemp Seeds

- 2 Tbsps. Dark Chocolate (Low Carb)

- 1/2 Cup Almond Milk

- 1 Tbsp. Cocoa Powder

- 2 Tbsps. Powdered Erythritol, To Taste

- Flake Salt, To Taste

- 1 Cup Ice

Method

1. Put the cocoa powder, hemp seeds, erythritol, and dark chocolate in a blender and mix until the chocolate is chopped.

2. Add the remaining ingredients and blend for a minute or two until a smooth consistency is attained.

3. Pour in the serving glasses and enjoy.

Keto Meal Replacement Shake

Servings: 2 | Time: 5 mins | Difficulty: Easy

Nutrients per serving: Calories: 453 kcal | Fat: 42.6g
| Carbohydrates: 6.9g | Protein: 8.8g | Fiber: 8.1g

Ingredients

- 1/2 Avocado

- 2 Tbsps. Almond Butter

- 1 Cup Almond Or Coconut Milk, Unsweetened

- 1/4 Tsp. Vanilla Extract

- 1/2 Tsp. Cinnamon, Powdered

- 2 Tbsps. Golden Flaxseed Meal

- 1/8 Tsp. Salt

- 2 Tbsp. Cocoa Powder

- 1/2 Cup Heavy Cream

- 15 Drops Liquid Stevia

- 8 Ice Cubes

Method

1. Combine all the ingredients in a blender and blend for a minute or two until a smooth consistency is attained.

2. Serve in the glasses and enjoy.

Keto Iced Coffee

Servings: 1 | Time: 5 mins | Difficulty: Easy

Nutrients per serving: Calories: 160 kcal | Fat: 16.1g | Carbohydrates: 1.5g | Protein: 1.6g | Fiber: 0g

Ingredients

- 3 Tbsps. Heavy Cream

- 5 Drops Liquid Stevia

- 1 Cup Brewed Coffee

- 1/2 Tsp. Vanilla Extract (Optional)

- Ice Cubes, To Taste

Method

1. Brew your coffee according to your preference and let it cool down to room temperature.

2. Combine the coffee with all the other ingredients in a blender and blend for about a minute or until it becomes frothy.

3. Pour the iced coffee in your favorite mug and enjoy.

Keto Pumpkin Cheesecake

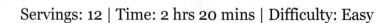

Servings: 12 | Time: 2 hrs 20 mins | Difficulty: Easy

Nutrients per serving: Calories: 242 kcal | Fat: 23g |
Carbohydrates: 5.7g | Protein: 6.5g | Fiber: 1.5g

Ingredients

- 3/4 cup Monkfruit

- 2/3 Cup Canned pumpkin

- 2 large eggs, at room temp

- 16 Oz Full fat cream cheese, at room temperature (2 blocks)

- 1 Tbsp Vanilla extract

- 1 Tbsp Pumpkin Pie Spice

- 1 Gluten-free Graham Cracker Crust, baked in a 9-inch springform pan

1. Preheat up to 325 °F in your oven.

2. Beat the cream cheese and the monk fruit together in a large bowl using the electric hand mixer until smooth and well mixed.

3. Include all the ingredients, then beat until they are mixed. Don't beat it too hard, or the entrance of too much air in the cheesecake will cause it to sink during baking.

4. With 2 or 3 layers of tinfoil, take the graham cracker crust first from the freezer and then wrap the bottom and the sides very firmly. Place the pan in a large pan for roasting.

5. Onto the crust, pour the cheesecake, and smooth out uniformly. Switch to your oven's middle rack and cover the pan with water until the springform pan comes halfway up.

6. Bake for about 55-60 minutes, until the outside is set and a little circle in the middle is jiggly. Turn the oven off and gently break the lock, allowing the cheesecake to sit for 15 minutes in the oven. Shift to the counter to cool fully, then.

7. Cover up and refrigerate for 8 hours until cool, but better if overnight.

8. Hover a knife down the sides of a cheesecake softly, cut the pan and slice it out.

Sugar-Free No-Bake Keto Cheesecake

Servings: 2 | Time: 5 mins | Difficulty: Easy

Nutrients per serving: Calories: 292 kcal | Fat: 28g | Carbohydrates: 4.9g | Protein: 8g | Fiber: 0.9g

Ingredients

For The Crust:

- 1 tsp Powdered Erythritol Sweetener (I used Swerve)

- 2 tsp Ghee or butter, melted

- 3 Tbsp Almond flour, packed

The Cheesecake:

- 0.5 Cup Cream cheese (softened to room temperature)

- 0.5 tsp Vanilla extract

- 8-12 tsp of Powdered Erythritol Sweetener (to taste)

- 4 Tbsp 2% Plain Greek yogurt

Method

1. Stir the almond flour with sweetener together in a shallow dish. In the ghee, add in and mix until crumbly. Push a tiny ramekin onto the rim.

2. Beat a cream cheese plus sweetener in a medium bowl using the electric hand mixer. Add Cream cheese and vanilla, then beat until mixed again, keeping the sides from scraping as desired.

3. To taste sugar again. Spoon over crust and smoothly spread out. To firm up cream cheese, cool for at least 2 hours.

Sugar-Free Keto Lemon Bars

Servings: 16 | Time: 1 hr 25 mins | Difficulty: Easy

Nutrients per serving: Calories: 106 kcal | Fat: 8.9g | Carbohydrates: 4.7g | Protein: 2.5g | Fiber: 2.3g

Ingredients

For The Crust:

- Pinch of salt

- 2 Tbsp Monkfruit

- 1/2 cup Coconut oil

- 1 cup of Coconut flour (95g)

For The Topping:

- 3/4 Cup Fresh lemon juice (about 6 large juicy lemons)

- 1 1/2 tsp Coconut flour, sifted

- 1/2 cup Monkfruit

- 2 tsp of Lemon zest

- 4 Eggs

Method

1. Preheat oven to 350 °F and use coconut oil to generously oil an 8x8 inch pan. Only put aside.

2. Include the coconut flour until it forms a dough.

3. Press the dough uniformly into the pan and bake for about 10 minutes, until just slightly golden brown.

4. Carefully stir together the lemon zest and eggs in a wide bowl until the crust has cooled.

Keto Brownies

Servings: 16 | Time: 30 mins | Difficulty: Easy

Nutrients per serving: Calories: 107 kcal | Fat: 10g | Carbohydrates: 5.7g | Protein: 2.5g | Fiber: 2.9g

Ingredients

- 1 large egg

- 1/2 tsp Baking soda

- 1/2 tsp Mint extract

- 1/4 cup Plant-based chocolate protein powder

- 1/4 tsp Sea salt

- 2 Egg yolks

- 2 Tbsp vanilla almond milk (Unsweetened)

- 5 ounces Sugar-free chocolate (roughly chopped and divided)

- 6 Tbsp Erythritol Sweetener

- 7 Tbsp Coconut oil (melted and divided)

Method

1. Preheat the oven to 350 °F and use coconut oil to generously oil an 8x8 inch pan. Put aside.

2. Beat the coconut oil and monk fruit and a pinch of salt together in a large bowl, using an electric hand mixer, until smooth and well mixed. Include coconut flour until it forms a dough.

3. Press the dough uniformly into the pan and bake for about 10 minutes, until just softly golden brown. Leave to cool for 30 minutes.

4. Lower the oven temperature to 325 °F and make sure that the oven rack is in the center of the oven.

5. Carefully stir together the lemon zest and eggs in a wide bowl until the crust has cooled. Don't use an electric blender here, or once fried, you can top with crack.

6. Heat the lemon juice softly in a separate, medium dish. Whisk in and stir in the monk fruit until it is dissolved. At room temperature, let it cool fully.

Peanut Butter Truffles

Servings: 10 Truffles | Time: 30 mins | Difficulty: Easy

Nutrients per serving (2 Truffles): Calories: 132 kcal | Fat: 9.9g | Carbohydrates: 10.9g | Protein: 4.4g | Fiber: 5.6g

Ingredients

- 2 tbsp Choc Zero Vanilla Syrup (Sugar-Free)

- 1/4 cup peanut butter

- 1/4 cup Coconut flour

- 1/3 cup chocolate chips (sugar-free)

Method

1. Mix all the peanut butter and the sugar-free syrup in a medium-sized dish.

2. To mix, add the coconut flour and mix. You are looking for a quality that you can roll into balls quickly. You can change the consistency if it is too moist or too dry by adding more coconut flour or the sweetener if required.

3. Take heaped Tsp. fuls of the blend and roll between your hands into balls. Move them to a plate or tray lined with paper that is oil proof.

4. Place the truffles for 10-20 minutes in the freezer until they are solid.

5. Melt the chocolate chips, meanwhile.

6. Take the truffles from the fridge and use the chocolate to decorate them. You should dip them in full or drizzle on top with a little chocolate-up it's to you.

7. For up to 1 week, you can store it in the refrigerator.

Creamy Keto Chia Pudding

Servings: 2 | Time: 6 hrs 10 mins | Difficulty: Easy

Nutrients per serving: Calories: 258 kcal | Fat: 18g | Carbohydrates: 8.15g | Protein: 3.66g | Fiber: 4.3g

Ingredients

- 1 cup Coconut milk full-fat

- 1 dash Salt

- 1/4 tsp Vanilla extract

- 1/4-1/2 tsp Stevia glycerite

- 2 tbsp Sugar-free jam

- 3 tbsp Black chia seeds

Method

1. In a small mug, mix the chia seeds and 1/2 cup of coconut milk.

2. Whisk together the vanilla, salt, and the leftover coconut milk. Use your preferred liquid sweetener to sweeten the flavor.

3. After 30 minutes, refrigerate and stir well to avoid Chia seeds from clumping at the bottom of the container. Overnight, refrigerate.

4. Layer the chia pudding in a serving cup or a small compact container of 1 Tbsp.   of sugar-free jelly. Store in your refrigerator for up to 5 days.

Salt And Pepita Hard Boiled Egg Snack

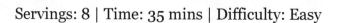

Servings: 8 | Time: 35 mins | Difficulty: Easy

Nutrients per serving: Calories: 94.5 kcal | Fat: 6.7g | Carbohydrates: 0.7g | Protein: 7.7g | Fiber: 0.3g

Ingredients

- 8 large Eggs

- 1 tsp Sea Salt

- 1/4-1/2 tsp Black Pepper (depending on you, how peppery you like your eggs)

- 1/4 cup Pepitas

1. Preheat to 400°F in your oven.

2. Place the eggs in the thin layer in a huge jar. Cover them and put them to a boil on high heat with 2 inches of water. Switch off the heat (but do not remove the pot from), cover and pot until they hit a rolling boil, and leave around 10-12 minutes. Pour the water and cover it with cold water, and let it stand for 10 minutes.

3. Place the pepitas over a small baking sheet while the eggs become fried and bake until softly golden brown, around 5-7 minutes.

4. Switch the toasted pepitas, pepper, and salt to the small food processor or the spice grinder and pulse until these broken down, but there are some small bits of texture.

5. By dipping into the mixture of pepitas, peel the eggs and DEVOUR

Crispy Air Fryer Brussels Sprouts

Servings: 4 | Time: 35 mins | Difficulty: Easy

Nutrients per serving: Calories: 78.2 kcal | Fat: 3.7g | Carbohydrates: 10.1g | Protein: 3.8g | Fiber: 4.3g

Ingredients

- Sea salt

- 1 Tbsp Olive oil

- 1 Lb Brussels sprouts

Method

1. Heat your fryer in the air to 350 F

2. Trim the ends of the sprouts in Brussels, cut the leaves and not look good. After trimming, you can end up with around 3/4 lb of the Brussels sprouts,

3. Place the Brussels in a bowl and toss with salt and olive oil. Remove and set aside any singular leaves for later.

4. Put the Brussels inside your air fryer's mesh basket and cook for about 12 minutes. Next, shake the basket, then cook for a further 10-12 minutes before you're done with the Brussels look. Put the singular leaves in the air fryer at this stage and cook for 2 to 3 minutes until crispy.

Sugar-Free Keto No Bake Cookies

Servings: 12 | Time: 10 mins | Difficulty: Easy

Nutrients per serving: Calories: 156.4 kcal | Fat: 14.4g | Carbohydrates: 5.7g | Protein: 3.8g | Fiber: 2.8g

Ingredients

- pinch of Salt

- 6 tbsp Almond Butter (the no-stir kind)

- 2 tbsp of Unsalted Butter (or dairy-free butter)

- 2 tbsp of Sugar-Free Chocolate Chips (or dairy-free)

- 2 1/2 tbsp Monkfruit Sweetener

- 1/2 cup Unsweetened Coconut Flakes

- 1 1/4 cups Almond Flour, (125g)

Method

1. Melt the almond butter & butter until they become smooth and creamy, around 1 minute, in a big, microwave-safe dish.

2. Whisk until it is absorbed in the monk fruit. Then stir in almond flour, the flakes of coconut, and salt.

3. To cool, put the bowl in the fridge for 15 minutes.

4. Whisk in the chocolate chips until cooled.

5. Roll into balls of 1 1/2 Tbsp and put on a cookie sheet lined with parchment paper. Slightly push out, to around 1/2 inch thick.

6. For at least an hour, cover and refrigerate.

Grilled Avocados With Feta Tahini Sauce

Servings: 6 | Time: 10 mins | Difficulty: Easy

Nutrients per serving: Calories: 199 kcal | Fat: 18.1g | Carbohydrates: 9.4g | Protein: 3.2g | Fiber: 6.2g

Ingredients

- 1 Garlic clove

- 2 tsp Fresh lemon juice

- 2 tsp Olive oil

- 3 Large Fresh Avocados

- Salt

For The Sauce:

- 1/4 cup Feta cheese, crumbled (37g)

- 1 1/2 Tbsp Tahini

- 1/2 - 1 Tbsp Reduced-sodium chicken broth (depending on how thick you like your sauce)

- 4 tsp Fresh lemon juice

- 1 tsp Honey

- Pinch of salt

Method

1. Preheat to medium-high heat on your barbecue.

2. Cut the avocados in half, and the seeds are removed. Peel a clove of garlic and take the top off. Everywhere on the cut side of avocado, rub the cut portion of the garlic.

3. In a shallow bowl, mix the olive oil and the lemon juice and spray over the avocados. Sprinkle salt on it.

4. Place the cut side down over the grill and cook for around 5-6 minutes before excellent grill marks are created.

5. Place the feta in the small microwave-safe bowl, then microwave it for about 10-15 seconds before cooking and softening, using a small food processor to mix all the sauce ingredients. To make sure it gets clean and creamy, you'll need to pause, scrape down each side, and then resume blending again—season with salt to taste.

6. Divide the sauce among the avocados, squeeze with the fresh lemon juice (not mandatory) and scoop to DEVOUR straight from the pod.

Keto Cucumber Salad

Servings: 4 | Time: 3 hrs 15 mins | Difficulty: Easy

Nutrients per serving: Calories: 49 kcal | Fat: 3.2g | Carbohydrates: 3.3g | Protein: 1.2g | Fiber: 0.7g

Ingredients

- 5 Tbsp Full-fat sour cream

- 2 tsp Fresh dill, minced

- 1 Large Cucumber, thinly sliced

- 1 1/2 Tbsp White vinegar

- 1 1/4 tsp Monkfruit Sweetener (you can use regular sugar too)

- 1/4 tsp Sea salt, or to taste

- 1/8-1/4 tsp Black pepper, to taste

- 1/4 of a Large Onion, sliced thinly

Method

1. In a big dish, blend all the ingredients until the cucumber is well combined.

2. Bring the cucumber & onions into the mixture and stir.

3. To produce flavors, cover, and refrigerate for about 3 hours.

Baked Zucchini Fritters

Servings: 16 | Time: 45 mins | Difficulty: Easy

Nutrients per serving: Calories: 222 kcal | Fat: 21.8g | Carbohydrates: 6.9g | Protein: 3.8g | Fiber: 2.8g

Ingredients

The Fritters:

- 1 cup Almond flour (100g)

- 1 Egg white

- 2 Tbsp of Olive oil, divided

- 2 tsp Coconut flour

- 2/3 cup diced Onion

- 20 Twists Real Salt Organic Garlic Pepper

- 3 Cups Grated zucchini, packed (2 large zucchinis)

- 20 Twists Organic Lemon Pepper Real Salt

- 3/4 - 1 tsp Real Salt Sea Salt

- 6 Tbsp Parsley, minced

- Olive oil spray

For The Dip:

- Real Salt Sea Salt, to taste

- 5 tsp Fresh lemon juice

- 4 Twists Real Salt Lemon Pepper

- 4 tsp Fresh dill, chopped and tightly packed

- 1/2 Cup Paleo-friendly Mayo

Method

1. Heat the oven to 400 °F. Line a parchment paper baking sheet. If you have one, use a dark-colored baking sheet as it helps crisp them

2. Place grated zucchini in the kitchen towel and apply as much moisture as possible to the loop. Put some muscle in it to keep the patties from becoming soggy. In a wide dish, add it.

3. In a wide skillet, heat 2 tsp of oil over medium heat and set aside the remainder for later. Cook the onion and add it to the zucchini until it's smooth and golden brown.

4. Add up all the Lemon pepper, parsley, salt, garlic pepper, coconut flour, and almond flour. Stir before it's blended properly. Add the white egg and cook until the zucchini is coated.

5. Drop 16 meager 1/4 cup balls on the baking sheet - or around 3 Tbsp. Push flat out (approximately 1/4 of an inch) and coat the tops with a spray of olive oil. (You would need to cook in two separate batches)

6. Bake for about 25-30 minutes, until the sides are golden brown as well as the top becomes slightly crispy. Then, change your oven to broil HIGH and broil for around 2-3 minutes until crisp. Look carefully at how they can burn quickly.

7. . Mix with all the dip ingredients and DEVOUR with fritters.

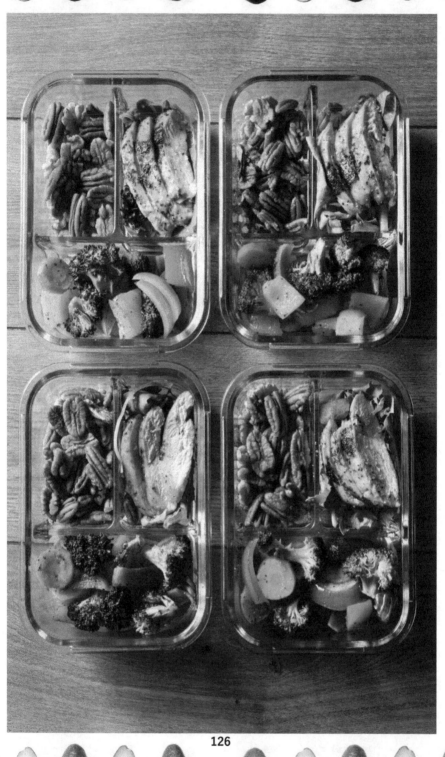

CPSIA information can be obtained
at www.ICGtesting.com
Printed in the USA
LVHW021535110521
687091LV00003B/323

9 781801 852531